M000012969

LORD

FORGIVE ME

I MARRIED THEM ALL!!!!

"If we confess our sins, he is faithful and he will forgive us of all our sins and purify us from unrighteousness."

— 1st John 1:9

ABBRA CHRISTOPHER

ISBN-13: 978-1-988439-34-1

Dedication

This book is dedicated to my (Mother) Alice Christopher and Robert Christopher (Father) they both passed early in life, while I was hurt, wounded, and broken, very angry at them both; because I needed them there to be parents, and they were absent. I felt it was due to their own selfish reasons, drug addiction, and alcohol. I thank God for blessing me with my grandfather (Lester Dorsey) and grandmother (Gertrude Dorsey) for raising me as their own into the strong woman that I have become. I am an overcomer through Jesus Christ my Lord and Savior. Thank you, Jesus, for growing me into the ordained woman you called me to be.

Special Acknowledgement

My Sons Alan and Aljuwon, who I had the pleasure of raising to the best I know. They have watched me go through all these trials and tribulations, while in these different marriages. I feel it has affected them as men growing up, mainly; they never had a stable male role model to lead them. Overall, today I have learned to trust God as their Father to lead and guide in this time of their life as young men. I am believing every day for a renewal of the mind and I declare that their life is being redeemed from destruction, I declare the blessing of God will operate in their lives daily, I declare that they will prosper and walk in the favor of God, I declare that my sons will grow strong in their intimacy with the Lord. I pray that God will send them a saved woman that has a relationship with Him, and will love them out of their hurt and pain. I love you both, my men of God!

Table of Content

Introduction

"If God is for us, who can be against us?" (Roman 8.31)

Minister Abbra is a woman of God, that has literally been married 6 times, and she plans to marry again for the 7th time with God's guidance. She will say she married most of her boyfriends, in her mind; she was trying to please her grandparents and God. She never read her word to show herself approved to be married; therefore, this caused a lot of trials and tribulations in each of these marriages. Though all of her issues and experiences, Minister Abbra had to go through the fire to receive deliverances. God had a plan to birth a word out of her to deliver a word for others to recognize their faults before marriage; no one can fix you, nor complete you. Sometimes, we lose ourselves and depend on a mate or a husband to make us happy, others can only enhance who you are. If you are wounded and broken, and it will destroy you and your marriage. God only design us to marry once only; but we do otherwise. We play the blame game; marriage is a representation of God's covenant here on earth. It is your responsibility to treat your mate right, don't worry about the other person in how they treat you; you will have victory at the end. It should be about your relationship with your Father in Heaven. You never allow anyone to dictate your happiness; you have to find happiness within yourself. Don't lose yourself in the relationship; find yourself by walking in your purpose. Take your mind off the problem and remember the promise that God said, (He ordain marriages), and you can do all thing through Christ. Minister Abbra has a gift that she didn't know what to do with it. The gift to have a husband, every woman or man has this gift also, if you desire it. You see God gave her beauty for her ashes; (Isaiah 6.13). It is her mess that has caused her to be the woman she is today.

Minister Abbra prays this book will help others to identify who they are before saying I do, and those that are married and looking for answers. She believes you can have a prosperous and victorious marriage if you take the authority God gave you. This is her prayer for you.

Chapter 1

MY PAIN

As a young girl, I grew up remembering my mother telling me I looked at life as a fairy-tale, and that it was as though it was… bed of roses, at that time, I didn't understand, but basically, it meant that I wanted everything to be perfect. I wanted love; I wanted the total opposite of what I had seen while growing up as a young girl. I was determined to set the right example for my sibling, because I was the oldest. You see my mother and father didn't raise me. My parents were drug-addicts and alcoholics, and left my grandparents to raise all 6 grandchildren. My grandparents did the best they could, but I never experience emotional, nor affectionate love, or a father love, or nutrient from a mother. My grandmother only knew to show us how to survive, by giving us shelter, clothes, and making sure we were well taken care of. In her eyes, we had the best, but we lack the most important thing, we needed in life, and that was showing us how to love one another and have a strong loyalty connection as sibling, my grandmother was a very strong woman; therefore, when I began to grow up as a young woman, I became strong, but I wanted love so bad, I began looking for it in all the wrong places. Any man that showed me any type of affection, you become my boyfriend and shortly afterwards my husband. I realized that I married all my long-term boyfriends, 1st marriage turned into 6 husbands. One would say why you had to marry them all; you could have just dated and lived together. There are several reasons; I felt if I married them all, they would never leave me like my parents. I also always tried to be a good girl, I always listen to my elders, I had a big mama that gave good advice, I remember her saying to me, why buy the cow if you can get the milk free, in other words, if you are going to have sex, then you need to marry them, this is what the bible tells us. So, I married them all. I also enjoyed sex so much in my mind, if I got married, this would somehow please God and my parents, I can enjoy sex while being married, and I mean the Bible clearly tells us it is better to marry than to burn. (1 Corinthians 7:9) But my heart was also starving for emotional love, as I continued to look for love in all the wrong places. I have experienced every type of man there is, I was very insecure, and I realized that I needed a daddy love from them. So, when time got rough in the marriage, I had a lot going on within my spirit, you see, I didn't know what marriage was, nobody ever explained this whole concept of what comes with it. I thought it was going to be easy like dating my boyfriend, whether he loves me or he loves me not. So, when the problems arrived, I left the marriage and went out and preyed on the next victim, The Funny thing is; I was attracting who I was, they were just the opposite sex. These sins cause me to hurt others not internally, but I carried my curses into each relationship, over and over again. I was hurting and didn't realize how I was hurting others as well, I preyed on these men's emotions, and this is why it was so easy to leave my marriage. I needed the love from my parents that I didn't get, so I turned to men instead. They were only crutches, and I was in bondages. I had a few good husbands; but they didn't know how to love either, they also were going through the emotions, once we both got tired of pretending, we both walked away confused. We both walked away broken, and wounded, and lost. These were generation curses that neither one of us, had not dealt with. We were all lost in our identity, we had no clue as to who we are, but yet married. So, follow me through my pattern of loss in my identity.

Chapter 2

YOU ATTRACT WHO YOU ARE

My first husband was my life savior in my mind; we were married for 5 years. It was supposed to be like a fairy tale, prince charming, just like my mother said. He was the one that was going to marry me and move me out of my parents' house, he was a military man and this would allow me to travel, and get away from living in the house with my grandparent. In this marriage, he gave me my 1st son, you see, I found later after getting married that it wasn't really a fairy tale, because I really didn't know what I wanted, I wasn't in love. Having to help with my 5 little siblings and work, and school, trying to also help my grandmother in any way I could, while my mother was out in the streets on drugs and my daddy an alcoholic, I thought this was the answer, only to find out my husband was an alcoholic too, a curse came from his father, he also was broken, because most of the time, we wouldn't talk about our issues, because we were young. It's as though we didn't exist to one another, and me not knowing, what my idea of a man was. My father and grandfather were both alcoholics as well. My husband was showing me the signs of being an alcoholic while we were dating in school, before marriage, I ignored it, due to wanting the security of having someone there, that cared, and not to be alone. The drinking only escalated when we got married. In my mind, he was going take me away and I would live happily ever after. I found later that I wasn't happy and I needed more, he just could not give me what I wanted, the sad part is, I didn't know what that was at that time, I always felt alone and lost. I finally left the marriage, still confused and broken, on a searching prey for my next victim to marry.

The second husband was a sugar daddy to me, we stayed married for 6 months, why I married him is because he was 20 years older and mature and reminded me of a father figure, he showered me with money and material things also; gave me anything I ask for, this marriage lasted only 6 months, because he became very possessive, and very controlling, started treating me like I was his child. For a while, I felt this was okay, I didn't know I was being emotionally abused, because he was showing me some type of love, but he was so controlling, and jealous, he went everywhere with me, and this drove me crazy! I found out later he had low self-esteem due to no education, and being in prison for as many as 20 plus years, which affected him mentally. He didn't grow up with his parent, they died while he was away, he was just basically looking for some type of fantasy and fell in love with a young girl, and he didn't know how to love. I allowed this as long as I could, and realize this is not how

I wanted to be loved and no money was going to make me happy. I left him with no remorse only to find my next victim.

Husband three was a playboy, the bad boy! We were married for 7 years; we had a son together. He cheated basically while we dated and in the entire time we were married. He was very controlling mentally and emotionally abusive. I basically loved his good look and his charm and he was fine. I realized I never really was in love with him, I didn't even love myself, because if I did, I wouldn't settle for the lies and the cheating all those years, I was only in love with the material things he offered. My husband experienced a lack of love from his parents, I remembered he had no real relationship with his father or mother, and there were always unsettling disagreements between his siblings, that wasn't normal. With this lust for women behavior, this made me feel, he didn't like women somehow. He felt loving me was having sex every time he wanted it, that was the good life for him; but yet I have to deal with all his games and be a good humble wife. I feel he made me his crutch while searching for his identity within his self, because even after filing for a divorce, he would stalk me and tell me if I can't have you no one would. He would blame his cheating and lies on having some type of addiction. When I left this marriage, I became even more wounded and broken, I left very angry! But it never stopped me from moving to my next victim.

Husband four was the little boy toy that rescued me, we stayed married for 4 years; He made me feel like a young girl that was dating, so it was exciting. He was 10 years younger than me and I wanted to have fun and date, something I had missed as a young adult growing up. I was 37 years old and he was 27 years old. To him, I was that older woman that made him feel like a man. He lost his mother at a young age, while his grandmother raised him. He had 2 small kids at an early age, and he still was a young man searching for his identity. We were both looking for something that we felt we could give to one another and that was love. We both had such low self-esteem; he was broken from a mother and a father's love. Both our mothers died and although his father was living, he always said his dad was dead to him, because his father never tried to have a relationship with him. You see, we had something in common; we both just wanted a different type love, so when the fun ran out and reality kicked in, we both realized it wasn't enough to stay together, and there was no real love. He cared for me, but it just wasn't enough. I remembered, he said in a counseling session that he wasn't sure if he really loved me, and that he never knew what love really was, I was okay with that, because I was lost as well, so I guess you could say I was looking for love in all the wrong places.

Husband five was a manipulator and a drug-addict, he seems like he had it going on, but he was a deceiver and a liar. We were married for 1 year. At that time, I was looking for financial gain and it wasn't about love... period. He portrayed himself as a charmer, and a moneymaker. I found later that he also was looking for the same thing, He was looking for financial gain, though me, I was the stable one with an upcoming business, his mother was deceased also, and he was still hurting from her death, she was all he talked about. She appeared to be his crutch; he wasn't close with his father. I found later that he had been struggling for a while and also hurt and broken from a previous ex-wife cheating on him. He was never in love with me, he had too much pain, only his drug substances that he was addicted to could help him, which kept him broken and telling lies. Our entire marriage was a lie; I guess we preyed on one another.

Husband six was the best friend that I never should have married. We had been friends since high school and always kept in touch, we knew a lot about each other's failed relationships, but we never talked about our childhood experiences, until we got married. On the outside amongst others, he portrayed himself as always happy, but behind closed doors, he had a dark side of him. This dark side caused him to be a drug addict and alcoholic. We were married for 2 years, I found that he was wounded and broken, but I married him anyway, thinking I could change him; but how could I change him, and I was still broken and still trying to find myself. His brokenness all came from being abused in childhood by his father and supporting his mother; because his older sibling was often incarcerated. He was angry at his mother and father and this caused him to not really like himself. This caused a lot of burden and resentment, being the youngest. Although he was a recovery addict and alcoholic, this angry affected us in the marriage. He would go for days and not talk to me, I knew this was a form of abuse, and this curse was a pattern in my life. He was also lost in his identity, we both needed help, but we just didn't know how to save one another.

Chapter 3

WHEN YOU THINK YOU ARE HEALED THE DEVIL WILL DECEIVE YOU

After my sixth divorce, I left so broken and needing clarity on why I can't keep my marriage together and how it was so easy to walk away... I had no clue. I needed to find who I was and get some understanding. I began attending therapy sessions and started my healing, and found that I was really angry with both my parents. I gained a more intimate relationship with my savior. In all of this process of getting to know me, I was saved by GRACE. I stayed single, getting to know myself for several years; I never gave up on wanting to one day after my healing to find true love. Well, I met Mr. nice guy, I thought he was my knight and shining armor. He was a charmer and a good-looking man, Rico Suave! He treated me like a queen for 3 years to be exact. It was the best relationship that I had since my healing and my deliverance from being broken. It felt so good to be in love and be loved, I knew without a doubt, because I knew who I was in Christ; therefore, it was easy to love back unconditional. I went in this relationship with my guards down, because of grace. Although, I knew I always wanted to be married, at this point, I was praying for God to show me, if this was my Boas, this guy was passing the test of everything that I desired in a husband, but I never stopped praying, you see warning come before destruction, when you are under God's Grace the devil will be exposed! I met his representative, he had a hidden agenda, but the devil got exposed quickly when he asked me to marry him after 2 years in the relationship. The devil knew I still wanted to be married, we know his ultimate goal is to steal, kill, and destroy! He sent his best.

He was a functional alcoholic that couldn't be tamed. This caused him to cheat and lie. By this time, I was madly in love with this man; I overlooked this issue, because of his attentiveness. I was deceived by the devil that used him to get my attention because; that demon spirit knew I wanted to be married again. Once he asked me to marry him, I prayed a little bit harder, because I needed a revelation, this could be my 7th husband, and I didn't want any more failed marriages. The Holy Spirit began to show me things quicker, He took the blinders off, and I began to see the light. The relationship changed, because all the negative things were being revealed right before my eyes, the lies and the cheating and the drinking were increasing. He also was dealing with deep-rooted issues from his childhood, a curse that followed him from a child to adult. He would always talk about how this bothered him; his father was an alcoholic and mistreated his mother with cheating and abusing her.

This affected all of his relationships tremendously. The Holy Spirit was showing me that this is your test, and you almost failed, are you ready to finally receive what God has for you? It's time for you to get out of the way Abbra, and allow God to send your mate. I had to allow God to order my steps. Sometimes God sends people in your life for a season and for a reason to help them or you to get through your issues. I will continue to pray for his deliverance, because he is a really good person, that needs healing, and I will always love him as a person, he was definitely part of my healing and my test to get to my destiny.

Chapter 4

LOST IN MY IDENTITY

The Bible tells us that our identity is accepting His gift of eternal life through faith. Jesus gave His life on earth and rose from the grave to conquer death and sanctify those who believe in Him; therefore, we are Christ-like and Christ lives in us. (Psalms 139:13 &14) "For it was you who created my inward parts; you knit me together in my mother's womb. I will praise you, because I have been fearfully and wonderfully made." When we become a believer of His word, we lose our identity in this world and embrace our identity in Christ. I became a very unhappy person, though all my marriage, my thinking was these men were going complete me. This incomplete spirit caused so much destruction in my life. This spirit caused me to hurt others as well; I carried this curse in all my marriages without knowing who I was. I didn't see the level of my self-esteem, this determined who I attracted. I was simply pimped by Satan; he used me, because I didn't want to be alone, so he tricked me into those marriages, the same type of spirit that attracted me. We attract who we are; he knew what the end was going to be. (John 10:10) "The thief comes only to steal and kill and destroy, but Jesus came that we may have life to the fullness," In order to bring about results to save my life. God had already provided everything I needed to have a healthy fulfilling relationship. As I began this mission, I realized before I received the husband God has for me, I must receive Him, I had to believe in His name, because He gave me those rights as His child, I must fall in love with my savior and myself. Once Jesus came on the scene I was no longer bound to sin and that even though I sinned I am under grace, although there were consequences for my actions. Believe me; I went through hell trying to find love in all the wrong places. Jesus died so that we will be free. No longer in bondage, I am the rightness of God, I am God's chosen child and He loves me so much that He gave His only son. (Galatians 3.26) when God created me, He created a masterpiece. I am the daughter of the living God. Knowing my identity is very important. I had no clue as to who I was. That little girl grew as an adult woman searching for her daddy's love and looking for the mother's nutrients and advice when I needed answers. My grandmother taught me how to be strong and get my own, and not to depend on anyone, but this has caused me to attract weak men and became the alpha woman in the relationship, because that's all I knew. **Genesis 1:** You see, in the beginning, God created man, and woman and the woman from the man ribs; therefore, the man is the head, led by God and woman is led by the man, just as

Christ is the head of the Church, which is the body of Christ. The only way to know who I was, was to study the word on who my savior said I am, The Bible tells us clearly to know the word for ourselves, and don't be deceived, many will perish without lack of knowledge. (Job 36.12). "I learned that Love is patient and kind, love does not envy or boast, it is not arrogant or rude, it does not insist on its own way. It is not irritable or resentful, it does not rejoice at wrongdoing but rejoices with the truth… love bears all things, believes all things, hopes all things, endure all things, and love never ends" **(1Corinthian 13:4,8)** I am grateful and saved by His grace. God has forgiven me for all my sins; I lacked wholeness because I was broken. I never got a chance to heal through each one of those relationships; therefore, carried all my curses in each one of those relationships. (The world calls it baggage) The way God intended for us to love is a wonderful thing, He wants us to enjoy life and be happy, being happy is falling in love with yourself and enjoying all God promises so you can reach and find, and enjoy your purpose and walk in your destiny.

Chapter 5

SOUL TIES

The Bible tells me, sin will have no dominion over me, since we are not under the law, but under grace, when Jesus came on the scene 2000 years ago, He said it is finished. He bored all my sins and I am now free. Are we to sin because we are not under the law, the answer is no. If I present myself to someone as an obedient slave, I am a slave to the one who I obey. I was a slave to sex. I mentioned earlier that one of the reasons I wanted to marry was for sex. Even though the bible clearly tells if we are lusting for sex, then we should have our own (husband). This was the most important reason for marrying, because I didn't want my grandmother to know I was having sex before marriage. I needed to be set free and out of bondage. **(John 8.32)** "And you know the truth; the truth will set you free. The curses that were keeping me bounded and broken have to have a deep cut in my spirit, because some would think, just because you get saved, you automatically have a relationship with God, or you delivered or you should know. The truth is; you have to be born again, and allow the Holy Spirit to guide you and the blinder will come off and look within your spirit and cut all those deep demons that still dwell in you, which include fornication, adultery, lust, and brokenness. **Psalm 40:13** "Lord please rescues me! Come quickly Lord and help me. I thank God that I am no longer a slave to the enemy, because I have been set free! I became a slave of unrighteousness." There is a clear warning against fornication in the scripture. When you unite yourself with another in a sexual manner, it's known that the two will become one flesh; it is also call sexual immorality. This is why the Bible instructs you not to have sex before marriage, because when you are having sex, your flesh is connecting and once the man penetrates and ejaculate inside you as a woman, it connects your sprit instantly, which is the blood, and the blood has a strong connection. Remember the blood of Jesus is what connects us to Him; this is why we love our Father in Heaven without even seeing Him in the nature; because he shaded His blood for us. **Hebrews 9:12** "the blood of Jesus makes a way for sinful man to be reconciled to a holy, perfect, just, and righteous God. **Hebrews 9: 22** "In fact, according to the law of Moses, nearly everything was purified with blood. For without the shedding of blood, there is no forgiveness. This is because the life is in the blood. When you, as a woman are, is pregnant you have an instant connection with your baby that you are carrying, this is due to the umbilical cord that connects the baby to your placenta, which carries blood from the uterus, and you fall in love with this baby that you have never seen. This is how it is when you have sex with a man, how he can easily get up and leave and never call are see you again, because he left all his bloodline (curses) with you. Now, he has moved onto his next soul tie (victim). There was a time when I was embarrassed, when someone would ask me why did I get married so many times, and I would ask them the same question, because every man you have sex with is your husband. As a reminder, this is one of the blessings of how our Father in Heaven consummate our marriages, through the blood. **Genesis 2**, "They shall be joined together, and they shall become one flesh. So, I had to remember that every man I had ever had sex with was also my husband, and this is one of the reasons, why I chose to marry **Corinthians 7:9**," It's better to married than to burnt. I basically knew I had a desire for sex, I just didn't believe that God created me to be a nun. I had all these feelings and it clearly states in the scripture that He didn't make man to be alone, **Genesis 2:18**, "Then, the Lord said, it's is not good for the man to be alone. I will make a helper who is just for me; therefore, if we must have these desires we should have our own husband, **1ˢᵗ Corinthians 7:2**, "Because of the temptation to sexual immorality, each woman should have their own husband." Was I wrong to think like this? Yes! I had the wrong interpretation of what the Bible indicated. I had the right concept, but the wrong perception. I wasn't told that marriage is a union that God joined together, not man. He gives the tools to prepare us for this day, and while you wait, you work on yourself to receive the man God has for you. Continue to study scriptures on marriage, pray, be watchful, while you are falling in love with you, to become the perfect wife that God has created you to be, I now know you don't wait till you get married, you start while you are singly-acting like a Godly wife, being a good wife isn't about being perfect. From a Christian standpoint, it's about striving to conduct you as a wife in a way that is pleasing to the Lord. So, when your mate comes and finds you, while you are preparing for him, you will have a disconcerting spirit and know instantly. He will not complete you, but enhance you! Remember no one has the power to complete, you but God and you. A good wife demonstrates an act of love to her husband, even when she feels he doesn't deserve it. **Proverbs 18:22** "Whosoever findeth a wife findeth a good thing, and obtained favor of the Lord." I had to realize that God didn't need any help for me. I never seek God before I got married; while I found this was so important because of all the mistakes that were made. I was incomplete and I felt another human being a (man) could do what God's role is! I missed so many blessings, just by not knowing the plan for my life.

Chapter 6

HEALING AND RESTORATION

When I began to define healing, it's the process of becoming healthy or restored, which is the action of repairing of fixing, or mending something. This is what I ask God to do; **Psalm 23:** "He restored my soul, He leadth me in the paths of righteousness for his name's sake." He Healed me. **Isaiah 53:5** "He said it's by his stripes I am healed I needed his help to walk through the journey without making the same mistakes. I needed a total transformation, bounty, and instructional in my life so the healing could begin. The Bible tells us **Psalm 107: 20** "he sent his word and healed them and delivered them from their destruction." **Psalm 107.20** "Submit yourself, therefore, to God, resist the devil and he will flee from you." I had to go to the valley to receive my healing. I know God anointed me and equipped me to go through all of my trials and tribulations, most women would not have been able to experience what I have been through, it is my mess that has grown me. Jesus said He will heal my heart, I needed emotional healing more than anything, the pain from being wounded and broken, even though I married these men without being in love, I was just going through the emotional roller coaster because I didn't want to be alone , and feel the pain of being hurt . I experience being in bondage over and over, I now know that God wants to prepare, so that when the time comes to receive my boas, I will be ready. I have heard people say that there is no guide to being married, who is not true, you have the Bible, the word has all the answers you need. **Proverbs 18.22** "He who finds a wife finds a good thing and obtains favor from the Lord." **Matthew 19:6** "So, they are no longer two but one flesh. Therefore, who

God has joined together let not man separate." **Proverbs 12:4** "and finally, I had no grounds for divorces, there was no sexual immorality. Lawfully in God's eye, I was still married to my last husband. **Matthew 5:32** "But I say to you that everyone who divorces his wife, except on the ground of sexual immorality, makes her commit adultery, and whoever marries a divorced woman commits adultery." If I knew what marriage was, I could have changed my husband by my walk, **1ˢᵗ Peter-3:1** "Wife, in the same way, submits yourselves to your own husbands, so that, if any of them do not believe the word they may be won over without words, but by the behavior of their wives." When they see the purity and reverence of your lives. **Proverb 12:4** "An excellent wife is the crown of her husband, but she who brings shame is like rottenness in his bones." **Isaiah. 61:3** "Christ gave me beauty for ashes; which means... he will take away the wounds, unhappiness, brokenness and makes my life beautiful. Did you know that when we need healing, it is hard for us to find peace of mind? When I received peace of mind and the knowledge of good health and knowing wholeness is His will for me, I can now enjoy my life free from unresolved conflicts and negative emotions that eat us alive inside and destroy our quality of life. Jesus puts all my broken pieces of life back together… little by little. Once I got this, I was able to now give him access to all my hurt and pain, and enable Him to heal me inside and out. Being healthy and whole means a lot to me, nothing is missing or broken in your mind, soul, spirit, or body. God replaced every missing piece, mended every broken place, and provided for every area of lack. The way God intended for us to love is a wonderful thing. A happy heart is a good medicine and a cheerful mind works healing, but a broken spirit dries up the bone, I feel being happy is a choice we make, and I know I choose to be happy! Just being whole and complete in myself, so when

I do meet my husband I will know, because I am confident in me, at this point, I only needed a husband to enhance me, not to complete me! I am now delivered and now I am totally forgiven through grace. **Proverbs 31** "Father, I surrender to you all my hurt, pain, worry, doubt, fear, and anxiety, and I ask you to wash me clean. You see when I began to get deliverance; he began to elevate me to prepare for the fight and be skilled and know how to recognize my next husband, **2Corinthians 4:4**, "Spiritual blindness is far worse than physical blindness. **Act 26:18** "to open their eyes so that they may turn from darkness to the light and from the dominion of Satan to God that they may receive forgiveness of sins and an inheritance among those who have been sanctified by faith in me. God took the blinder and now I can see.

Chapter 7

FALLING IN LOVE WITH MY SAVIOR

"Love the Lord your God with all your heart, all your soul, and your entire mind."—Mark 12:30-31

As I define the word love, it is a feeling of a deep affection; it comes with conditions versus falling in love or an intense craving to be connected to something or someone without conditions. In order to fall in love with God, you can't have any distractions; the Bible has all you need to understand who you are. You have to read your word to find your purpose here on earth, so you have to study and show yourself approved (2 Timothy 2.15), the Holy Spirit will show you what you need to see and understand. Satan's target is your mind, Satan's weapon is lies, and Satan's purpose is to make you ignorant of God's Will. I often wondered where I can find my place in God's story, God's purpose for my life should be the heartbeat that pumps through everything I do. What I learn in order to disconcert God's purpose sometimes, the best place to look for guidance is in your past; remember your past is what has made you who you are. Although I was saved and Christ lives in me, I didn't have an intimate relationship with him, it was all learned behavior, I had a friendship with him, but I wasn't in love. You know how you can have a friendship with someone and have conditions, but as you spend time with that individual, you began to care more and start loving that person without conditions. This was why it was easy to give up on the marriage without seeking him first. I never loved them or myself, I walking around with anger and bitterness, and pretending to be happy, but I was so sad and broken inside. I needed to spend time with God to gain that relationship, in order to know Him;

otherwise, I would miss my purpose. I found that He loves me unconditionally, just as I should have loved my husbands, it wouldn't be so easy to break my vows if I had a true understanding, and consider Him first. You not only give vows to your husband, but God too, it takes 3 in a marriage. We can't abandon the very first love, this is God's expectation of any man I fall in love with. Anyone who does not know how to love does not love God unconditionally. He must be your first love. (1st John 4.8) God showed his love when he went to the cross for me. I believe anyone that will die for me to save me; he has to love me unconditionally. I am grateful and saved by His grace. I was too afraid to take my eyes off Him. It reminded me of the story of Peter when he was being swallowed by the whale, he got distracted, and took his eyes off Jesus, however, the whale spit him out, and he was given another chance. Once you find yourself in Christ and began to love you, then you can love others like Christ like. (John13:34), Jesus said, a new commandment I give to you, that you love one another, just as I have loved you. After I fell in love with God, I found out who I was, where I belong, He created me in His image, to prove His love, "Once Jesus came on the scene I was no longer bound to sin and even though I sinned I am not a sinner… I am under grace." Jesus died so we will be set free, no longer in bondage. There is darkness, not knowing your identity, I had no clue. I didn't realize that a learned behavior can transform into a curse. I thank God for Grace.

Chapter 8

WHO ARE YOU WHEN OTHERS SEE YOU?

It is important to confess my sins; I don't want to be like Sapphire the woman in the Bible that was married 7 times. It's not clear why she married 7 times, but she died married to the 7th husband. **Act 5: 10** "instantly, she fell to the floor and die due to a conviction. I am a whole new person in the body of Christ, prepared to receive another husband which will be #7 which means in the Bible, completion or perfection. **Genesis 1: 2:1-2** tells us that" God created the Heavens and the earth in six days, and rested the 7th day after completion; I am in a place where God's Spirit lives in me. I am God's incredible work of art; I am spiritually alive. I have become God's messenger to the world; I now know he used me to deliver truth. I am sharing my experience with you in hope you can learn something that will bless your life, you see it is Satan's ultimate goal to steal kill and destroy, it was all in Satan plan to destroy, he wanted to destroy me by continuing in a demon driven marriages that God had nothing to do with, by destroying my mind, self-esteem, rejection, brokenness. I was hidden in the valley for so long. When I gave him a yes, it was then time to give birth to release all my pain. As a Christian, I am aware that the blood of Jesus cancelled out all my sins debts and assigns me a new creation identity. **Psalm 139**," He created me to be fearfully and wonderfully made in the image.

Chapter 9

WAITING FOR MY BOAS

As I spoke earlier, I will get remarried again, why because this is my desire and it's what I believe. I want to please my Father in Heaven by not sinning and being obedient. **1ˢᵗ Samuel 15:22** "Obedience's is better than sacrifice." My destiny is not what I was taught because of learned behavior or curses that were placed on my life. I thank God as I release my faith to send the boas (husband) He has for me. There is no condemnation, **1ˢᵗ John 1:9** "If we confess our sins, he is faithful and he will forgive us of all our sins and purify us from unrighteousness, grace changed my life." I began to meditate on **2nd kings 5:10"** Elisha sent a messenger to say to him, go wash yourself 7 times in the Jordan River, and your flesh will be restored and you will be cleansed. God forgave me, but I had to forgive my parents and myself, I had to also ask for forgiveness my from ex-husbands, therefore, when I remarried, I will not carry curses in the marriage. When the time comes, I will be ready to receive the husband God has for me, I will be complete. I have defeated the giant that kept me in bondages. I am a newly changed woman with a new vision, the Bible tells us in **Proverb 31: 10** "Who can find a virtuous and capable wife; she is more than precious than rubies." My six sins are erased and forgiven, when Jesus died 2000 years ago, He said at the cross that it is finished, when he came back on the scene and rose again on the 7th day to pronounce that I am free, then He rested. He loved me just that much. Thank you Jesus for loving me, when I didn't even love myself. I am expecting Him to show out, and exceed my expectation! Hallelujah, I am forgiven.

Chapter 10

FOUR THING YOU MUST KNOW

1. **Honor your marriage** – The word honor means to highly value something, to appreciate, cherish and recognize it as a priceless treasure.

   1Peter 3:7 "In the same way you husbands must give honor to your wives. Treat your wife with understanding as you live together. She may be weaker than you are, but she is your equal partner in God's gift of new life. Treat her as you should so your prayers will be hindered."

2. **Patience** – A person's ability to write something out or endure something. You remain calm, even when you've been waiting forever or dealing with something painstakingly slow or trying to teach someone how to

do something and they just don't get it. It's a quality of self–restraint or of not giving way to anger,

Roman 15:5 "May God, who gives this patience and encouragement, help you live in complete harmony with each other, as is fitting for followers of Christ Jesus.

3. **Love unconditional** – Loving another human being in the same way that God loves us is a very unique kind of love. We should love with agape love, Love is patient, love_is_ Kind, Love does not envy, Love does not boast, Love is proud, Love does not dishonor others.

1ˢᵗ **John 4:8** "Anyone who does not love, does not know God, because God is love."

4. **Forgiveness** – Be kind and compassionate to one another, forgiving each other, just as Christ God forgave you.

If you forgive other people when they sin against you, your Heavenly Father will also forgive you. Bear with each other and forgive one another if any of you has a grievance against someone.

Genesis 50:17 I "ask you to forgive your brothers the sins and the wrongs they committed in treating you so badly. Now, please forgive the sins of the servants of God your father.

Remember your responsibility in your relationship is not to worry about the way you are being treated, but the way you treat them. It's not about you, but about the relationship with your father in heaven, because he is watching, and he will lead and direct you.

Chapter 11

JESUS CHRIST'S LOVE LETTER TO ALL THAT ARE BROKEN

My beloved child, you may not know me, as well as I know you; but I know everything about you. I know when you sit down and when you rise up, I am familiar with all your ways, even the very hairs on your head are numbered, for you are my offspring. I knew you even before you were conceived, I chose you when I planned creation. You were not a mistake, for all your days are written in my book, I determined the exact time of your birth and where you would live, you are fearfully and wonderfully made, I knit you together in your mother's womb and bought you forth on the day you were born, I have been misrepresented by those who don't know me, I am not distant and angry, but am the complete expression of love and it is my desire to lavish my love on you.... simply because, you are my child and I am your Father. I offer you more than your earthly father ever could, for I am the perfect Father, every good gift that you receive comes from my hand, for I am your provider and I meet all your needs. My plan for your future has always been filled with hope, because I love you with an everlasting love, my thoughts toward you are countless as the sand on the seashore, and I rejoice over you singing. I will never stop doing good to you, for you are my treasured possession, I desire to establish you with all my heart and all my soul, and I want to show you great and marvelous things. If you seek me with all your heart, you will find me. Delight in me and I will give you the desires of your heart. For it is I who gave you those desires. I am able to do more for you than you could possibly imagine, for I am your greatest encourager. I am the Father who comforts you in all your troubles when you are brokenhearted, I am close to you, as a shepherd that carries a lamb, and I have carried you close to my heart. I will wipe away every tear from your eyes, and I will take away all the pain you have suffered on this earth. I am your father and I love you even as I love my son, Jesus, through Jesus, my love you were revealed. He is the exact representation of my being. He came to demonstrate that I am for you, not against you, and to tell you that I am not counting your sins, Jesus died so that you and I could be reconciled. His death was the ultimate expression of my love for you. I gave up everything I loved that I might gain your love. If you receive the gift of my son Jesus, you receive me, and nothing will ever separate you from my love again. Come to me and I'll throw the biggest party heaven has ever seen. I have always been a Father, and will always be Father, my question is, and will you be my child? I love you!

PRAYER FOR THE BROKENNESS

Dear God, I come to you thanking you for the forgiveness of my sins, as I confess. I thank you as I walk in the authority you have given me to be delivered from my hurt and pain, I was broken and wounded, and now, I am healed. Thank you that I have been given the power and the anointed ability to get results. I am now made whole and complete in your name; I thank you Lord that I no longer have condemnation and shame because I am delivered and set free out of the hands of the enemy. I thank you for a renewing of my mind and your unmerited, favor and grace over my life. I am the righteousness of God; therefore, I declare and decree that everything I have asked in your name is done and I release my faith in the name of Jesus!

BIBLE REFERENCES

FORNICATION / ADULTERY

1st Corinthians 6:9-10 "Know ye not that the unrighteous shall not inherit the kingdoms of God? Be not deceived: neither fornicator, nor idolaters, nor adulterers, nor effeminate, nor abusers of themselves with mankind, nor thieves nor covetous, nor drunkards, nor revilers, nor extortions, shall inherit the kingdom of God."

Matthew 5:27, 28 "Thou shalt not commit adultery: But I say unto you, that whosoever looketh, on a woman to lust after her hath committed adultery with her already in his heart."

MARRIAGE

Genesis 2:18 "Then the Lord God said it is not good that the man should be alone; I will make him a helper fit for him."

Proverb 18:22 "He who finds a wife finds a good thing and obtains favor from the lord."

FORGIVENESS

Proverbs 17:9 "Love prospers when a fault is forgiven, but dwelling on it separates close friends."

Ephesians 4:32 "Be kind to one another, tender hearted, forgiving one another, as God in Christ forgave you."

ANGER

James 1:19-20 "My dear brothers and sisters, take note of this everyone should be quick to listen slowly to become angry, because human anger does not produce the righteousness that God desires."

Ecclesiastes 7:9 "Keep your temp under control it is foolish to harbor a grudge."

WITCHCRAFT SPIRITS

Galatians 5:2 "Worshiping Gods, doing witchcraft, hating, make trouble, being jealous, being angry, being self, and making people angry with each other, causing divisions among people."

1Chron.10:13 "Saul died because he was unfaithful to the Lord; he did not keep the word of the lord and even consulted a medium for guidance."

Exodus 20: 2 "I am the Lord thy God, thou shalt not have any gods before me.

GENERATIONAL CURSES

2 Corinthians 5: 17 "Therefore, if anyone is in Christ, the new creation has come. The old has gone, the new is here."

Galatians 3:13 "Christ redeemed us from the curse of the law by becoming a curse for us, for it is written. Cursed is everyone who is hung on a pole."

SPIRIT OF DECEPTION

Psalm 10:7 "His mouth is full of lies and threats; trouble and evil are under his tongue."

Psalm 36: 3 "The words of their mouths are wicked and deceitful; they fail to act wisely or do well."

Psalms 120:2 "Save me, Lord, from lying lips and deceitful tongues."

BROKENNESS

Isaiah 53:5 "But he was pierced for our transgressions, he was crushed for our iniquities; the punishment that brought us peace was on him, and by his wounds, we are healed."

LOVE

1 Corinthians 13: 1 "Love is patient, love is kind. It does not envy, it does not boast, it is not proud. It is not rude, it is not self-seeking, it is not easily angered, and it keeps no record of wrongs. Love does not delight in evil but rejoices with the truth."

IDENTITY

Genesis 1:27 "So God created mankind in own image, in the image of God he created them; male and female."

Roman 6:6 "For we know that our old self was crucified with him so that the body ruled by sins might be done away with, that we should no longer is slaves to sin."

WHOLENESS

Peter 5: 10 "And after you have suffered a little while, the God of grace, who has called you to his eternal glory in Christ, will himself restore, confirm, strengthen, and establish you."

RESTORED

Psalm 147:3 "He heals the brokenhearted and blinds up their wounds."

SOUL TIES

Ezekiel 18: 4 "Behold, all souls are mines; the soul of the father as well as the soul of the son is mine, the soul who sins shall die."

COMPLETENESS

James 1: 4 "So let it grows, for when your endurance is fully developed, you will be perfect and complete lacking nothing."

SEX IMMORALITY

Hebrew 13:4 "Let marriage be held in honor among all, and let the marriage bed be undefiled, for God will judge the sexually immoral adulterous.

ABOUT THE AUTHOR

Minister Abbra Christopher is a native of Atlanta, Georgia. She is very kind-hearted, who always consider others first before herself. She is presently unmarried and has been for 5 years. She has 2 sons and 4 grandchildren, who she adores.

Abbra has been active in ministry for 20 years; she has a Bachelor of Art of religion in Pastoral Care and is a certified Christian Counselor.

Abbra is the founder and CEO of Victim of Victory Outreach Ministry, since 2007. This agency is a nonprofit agency that provides advocacy and housing for the community that is homeless and caregiver for the sick and shut-in. She educates those who are less fortunate and provides them with a safe-haven.